LEVEL TWO

Hymns With Chords

arranged by
CAROLE FLATAU

AF732259

David Carr Glover METHOD for PIANO

CONTENTS

Abide with Me 2
All Hail the Power 3
Come, Thou Almighty King 4
Doxology 5
Fairest Lord Jesus 6
God Be with You 7
God Is So Good 8
Holy God, We Praise Thy Name 8
Holy, Holy, Holy 10
It Is Well with My Soul 11
Jesus Loves Me 12
Joyful, Joyful, We Adore Thee 13
Just a Closer Walk with Thee 14
Just As I Am 15
Lord, Dismiss Us with Thy Blessing 16
My Jesus, I Love Thee 17
Nearer My God to Thee 18
Near the Cross 19
O How I Love Jesus 20
Onward Christian Soldiers 20
O Worship the King 22
Stand Up, Stand Up For Jesus 23
Sun of My Soul 24
Sweet Hour of Prayer 25
This Is My Father's World 26
This Is the Day 27
We Gather Together 28
What a Friend We Have In Jesus 29
When He Cometh 30

Design : Jeannette Aquino
Editor: Carole Flatau

ABIDE WITH ME

H.T. LYTE

W.H. MONK
Arranged by CAROLE FLATAU

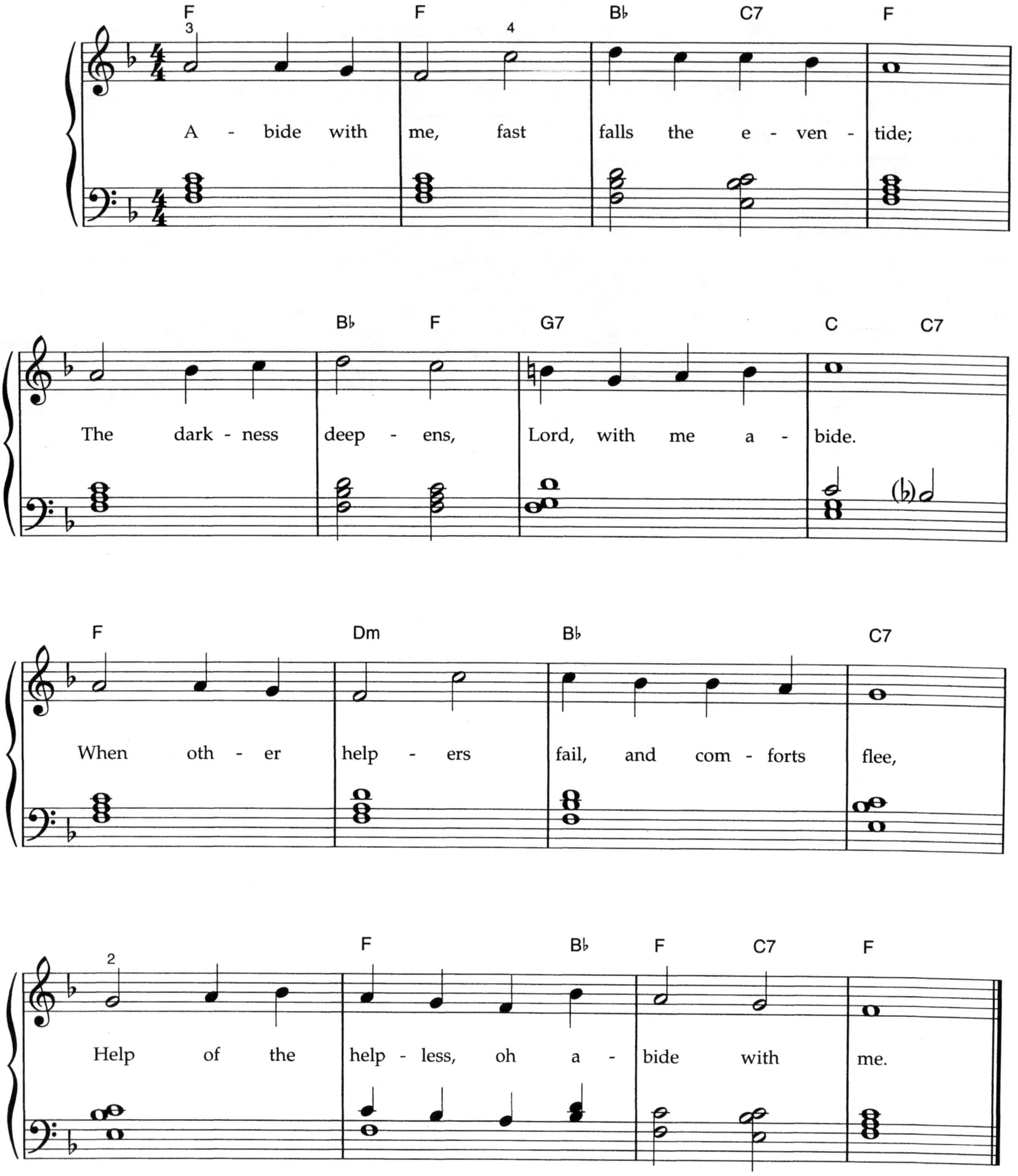
F F B♭ C7 F
A - bide with me, fast falls the e - ven - tide;
B♭ F G7 C C7
The dark - ness deep - ens, Lord, with me a - bide.
F Dm B♭ C7
When oth - er help - ers fail, and com - forts flee,
F B♭ F C7 F
Help of the help - less, oh a - bide with me.

FDL9501

ALL HAIL THE POWER

EDWARD PERRONET

OLIVER HOLDEN
Arranged by CAROLE FLATAU

F C7 F
All hail the pow'r of Je - sus name, Let an - gels pros - trate
F C7 F
fall; Bring forth the roy - al di - a - dem, And
G7 C F
crown Him Lord of all. Bring forth the roy - al
C7 F B♭ F C7 F
di - a - dem, And crown Him Lord of all.

COME, THOU ALMIGHTY KING

FELICE DE GIARDINI
Arranged by CAROLE FLATAU

G
D7
G
Come, Thou al - might - y King, Help us Thy
D7
G
name ___ to sing, Help us to praise;
D7
G
D7
G
Fa - ther, all glo - ri - ous, O'er all vic - to - ri - ous,
Come and reign o - ver us, An - cient of days.

DOXOLOGY
(Old Hundredth)

GENEVAN PSALTER
Arranged by CAROLE FLATAU

G
Praise God, from whom all bless - ings flow, Praise
C D7 G D7
Him, all crea - tures here be - low; Praise Him a - bove, you
C Em G D7 G D7 G
heav'n - ly host; Praise Fa - ther, Son and Ho - ly Ghost. A - men.

FAIREST LORD JESUS

CRUSADERS' HYMN
Arranged by CAROLE FLATAU

D
3
A7
2
D
1
Fair - est Lord, Je - sus, Rul - er of all na - ture,
A7
D
2
G
D
A7
2
3
O, Thou of God and ___ man the Son.
D
4
A7
4
Thee will I cher - ish, Thee will I
D
A7
D
hon - or, Thou my soul's glo - ry, joy and crown.

GOD BE WITH YOU

JEREMIAH RANKIN

WILLIAM G. TOMER
Arranged by CAROLE FLATAU

C G C F C
God be with you till we meet a - gain, By His coun-sels guide, up - hold you,
G C F G C
With His sheep se - cure - ly fold you, God be with you till we meet a - gain.
CHORUS
C F C
Till we meet, till we meet, Till we meet at Je - sus'
G F F C G7 C
feet, Till we meet, Till we meet, God be with you till we meet a - gain.

GOD IS SO GOOD

TRADITIONAL
Arranged by CAROLE FLATAU

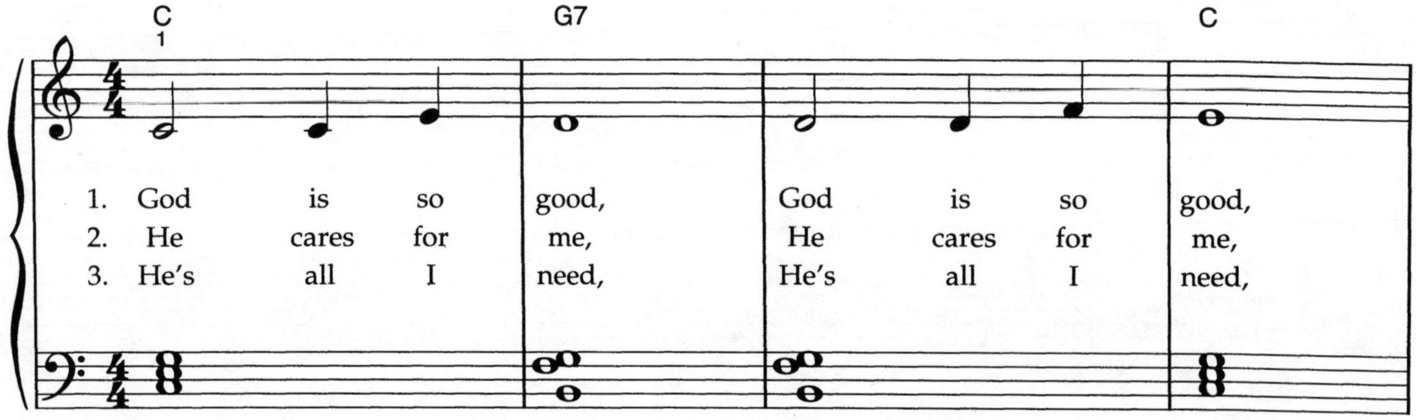
C
1
G7
C
1. God is so good, God is so good,
2. He cares for me, He cares for me,
3. He's all I need, He's all I need,

F
C
G7
C
God is so good, He's so good to me.
He cares for me, He's so good to me.
He's all I need, He's so good to me.

HOLY GOD, WE PRAISE THY NAME

from KATHOLISCHES GESANGBUCH
Arranged by CAROLE FLATAU

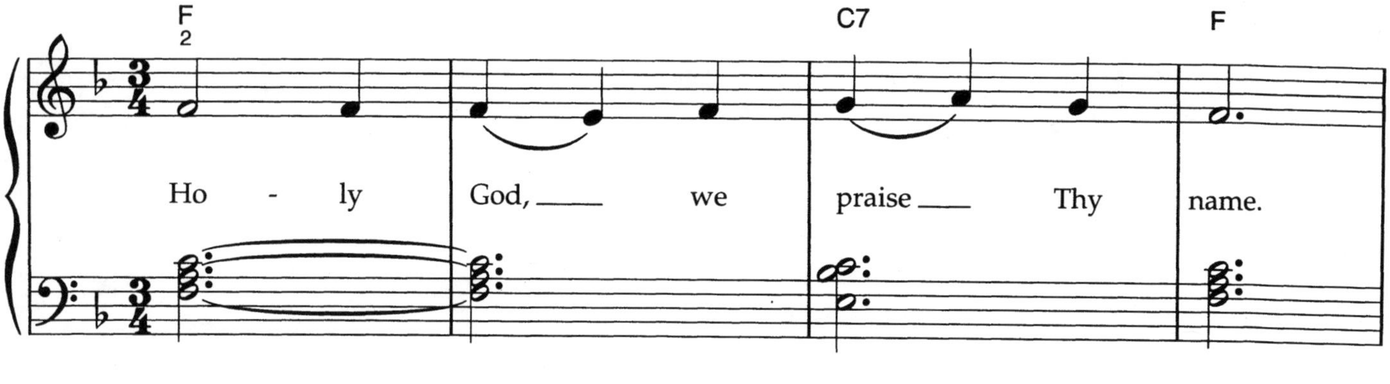
F
2
C7
F
Ho - ly God, we praise Thy name.

C
Lord of all we bow be - fore Thee.
F C7 F
All on earth Thy scep - ter claim,
C
All in heav'n a - bove a - dore Thee.
F
In - fi - nite Thy vast do - main,
B♭ F C7 F
Ev - er - last - ing is Thy reign.

HOLY, HOLY, HOLY

REGINALD HEBER

JOHN B. DYKES
Arranged by CAROLE FLATAU

C F C
Ho - ly, ho - ly, ho - ly, Lord God Al - might - y!
G C G D7 G G7
Ear - ly in the morn - ing our song shall rise to Thee.
C F C
Ho - ly, ho - ly, ho - ly, mer - ci - ful and might - y,
Am G7 C
God in Three Per - sons, bless - ed Tri - ni - ty.

IT IS WELL WITH MY SOUL

HORATIO G. SPAFFORD

PHILIP P. BLISS
Arranged by CAROLE FLATAU

C F C
1. When peace, like a riv - er, at - tend - eth my way, When
2. Tho Sa - tan should buf - fet, tho tri - als should come, Let
Am G C F
sor - rows like sea bil - lows roll, What - ev - er my lot, Thou hast
this blest as - sur - ance con - trol, That Christ hath re - gard - ed my
Dm G C G7 C
taught me to say, It is well, it is well with my soul.
help - less es - tate, And hath shed His own blood for my soul.
G C G G7
It is well with my soul,
C F C G7 C
It is well, it is well with my soul.

JESUS LOVES ME

ANNA B. WARNER

WILLIAM BRADBURY
Arranged by CAROLE FLATAU

C F C
Je - sus loves me, this I know, For the Bi - ble tells me so;
F C G7 C
Lit - tle ones to Him be - long, They are weak but He is strong.
CHORUS
F C G7
Yes, Je - sus loves me, Yes, Je - sus loves me.
C F C G7 C
Yes, Je - sus loves me The Bi - ble tells me so.

JOYFUL, JOYFUL, WE ADORE THEE

HENRY VAN DYKE

LUDWIG van BEETHOVEN
Arranged by CAROLE FLATAU

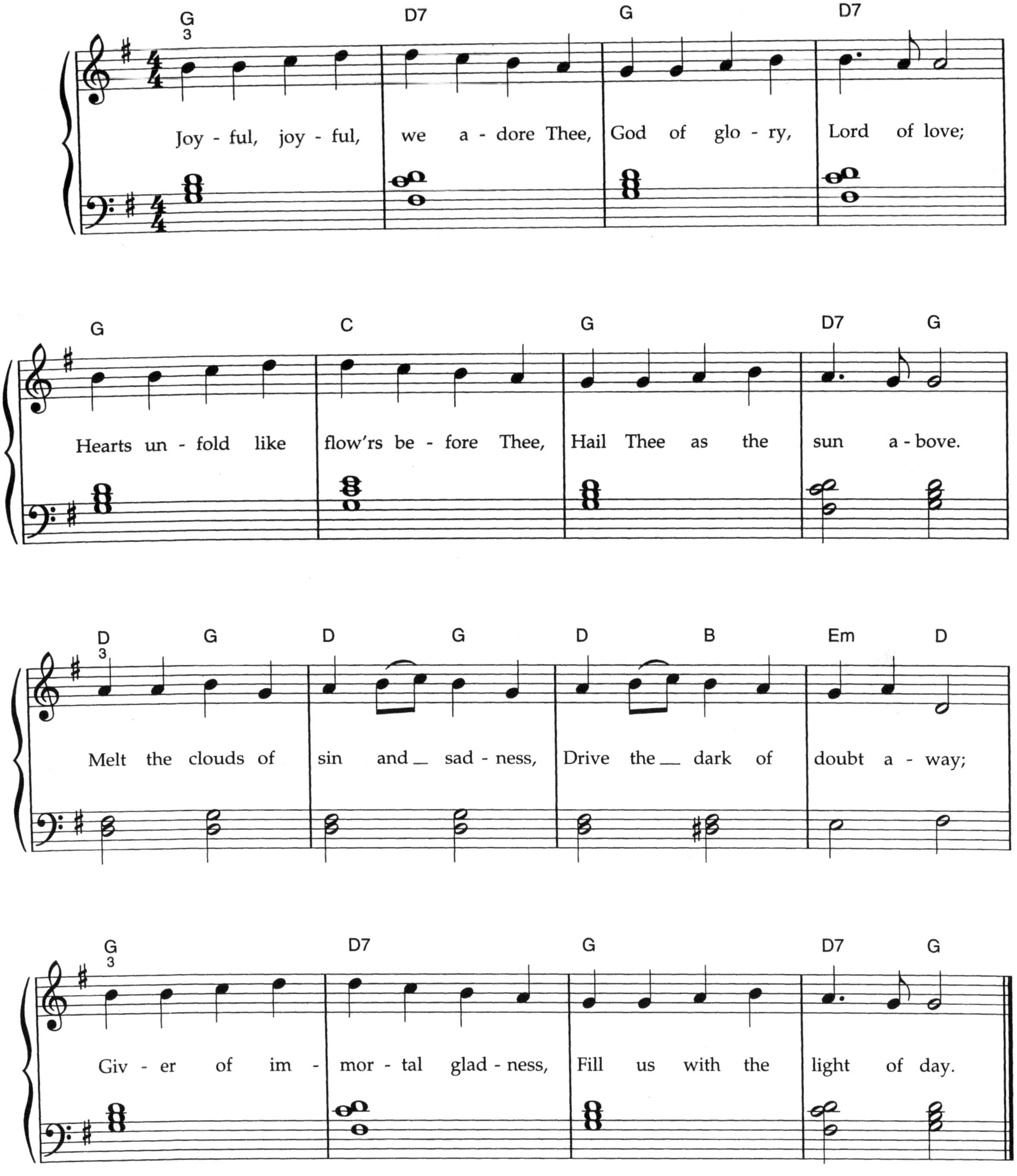
G D7 G D7
Joy - ful, joy - ful, we a - dore Thee, God of glo - ry, Lord of love;
G C G D7 G
Hearts un - fold like flow'rs be - fore Thee, Hail Thee as the sun a - bove.
D G D G D B Em D
Melt the clouds of sin and sad - ness, Drive the dark of doubt a - way;
G D7 G D7 G
Giv - er of im - mor - tal glad - ness, Fill us with the light of day.

JUST A CLOSER WALK WITH THEE

TRADITIONAL
Arranged by CAROLE FLATAU

B♭
F7
1. Just a clos - er walk with thee,
2. I am weak but Thou art strong,
3. When my fee - ble life is o'er,
E♭
B♭
Grant it Je - sus is my plea.
Je - sus keep me from all wrong.
Time for me will be no more.
E♭
Dai - ly walk - ing close to Thee, Let it
I'll be sat - is - fied as long, As I
Guide me gent - ly to that shore, Let me
B♭
F7
B♭
E♭
B♭
be, dear Lord, let it be.
walk, dear Lord, close to thee.
walk, dear Lord, close to thee.

JUST AS I AM

CHARLOTTE ELLIOT

WILLIAM BRADBURY
Arranged by CAROLE FLATAU

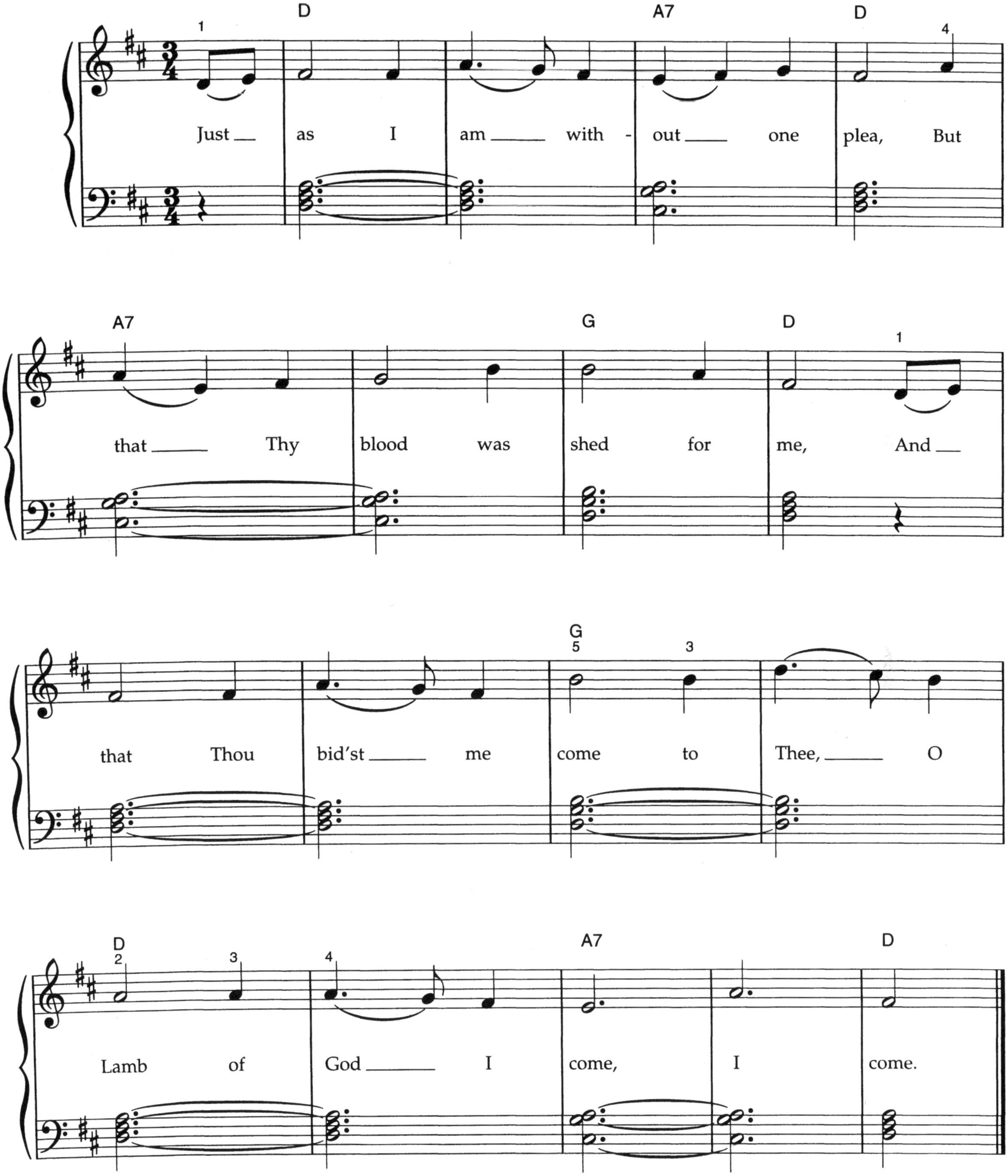
D A7 D
Just as I am without one plea, But
A7 G D
that Thy blood was shed for me, And
G
that Thou bid'st me come to Thee, O
D A7 D
Lamb of God I come, I come.

LORD, DISMISS US WITH THY BLESSING

SICILIAN MARINERS
Arranged by CAROLE FLATAU

C D7
Lord, dis - miss us with Thy bless - ing, Fill our hearts with
G D7 G C
joy and peace; Let us each, Thy love pos - sess - ing,
D7 G D G
Tri - umph in re - deem - ing grace; O re - fresh us,
C F C G7 C
O re - fresh us, Tra - vel - ing through this wil - der - ness.

MY JESUS, I LOVE THEE

A.J. GORDON
Arranged by CAROLE FLATAU

F B♭ F C7 F
My Je - sus, I love Thee, I know Thou art mine; For
B♭ F C7 F
Thee all the fol - lies of sin I re - sign. My
C7 F C F
gra - cious Re - deem - er, my Sav - ior art Thou; If
B♭ F C7 F
ev - er I loved Thee, my Je - sus, 'tis now.

NEARER, MY GOD TO THEE

SARAH ADAMS

LOWELL MASON
Arranged by CAROLE FLATAU

F Bb F
Near - er, my God, to Thee, Near - er to
C7 F Bb
Thee. E'en though it be a cross
F C7 F Bb
That rais - eth me. Still all my
F Bb F C7
song shall be, Near - er my God, to Thee,
F Bb F C7 F
Near - er, my God to Thee; Near - er to Thee.

NEAR THE CROSS

FANNY CROSBY

WILLIAM H. DONAE
Arranged by CAROLE FLATAU

F Bb F C7
1. Je - sus keep me near the cross, There a pre - cious foun - tain,
2. Near the cross, a trem - bling soul, love and mer - cy found me;
F Bb F C7 F
Free to all, a heal - ing stream flows from Cal - v'ry's moun - tain.
There the bright and morn - ing star sheds its beams a - round me.
CHORUS
F Bb F C7
In the cross, in the cross, be my glo - ry ev - er,
F Bb F C7 F
till my rap - tured soul shall find rest, be - yond the riv - er.

O HOW I LOVE JESUS

AMERICAN MELODY
Arranged by CAROLE FLATAU

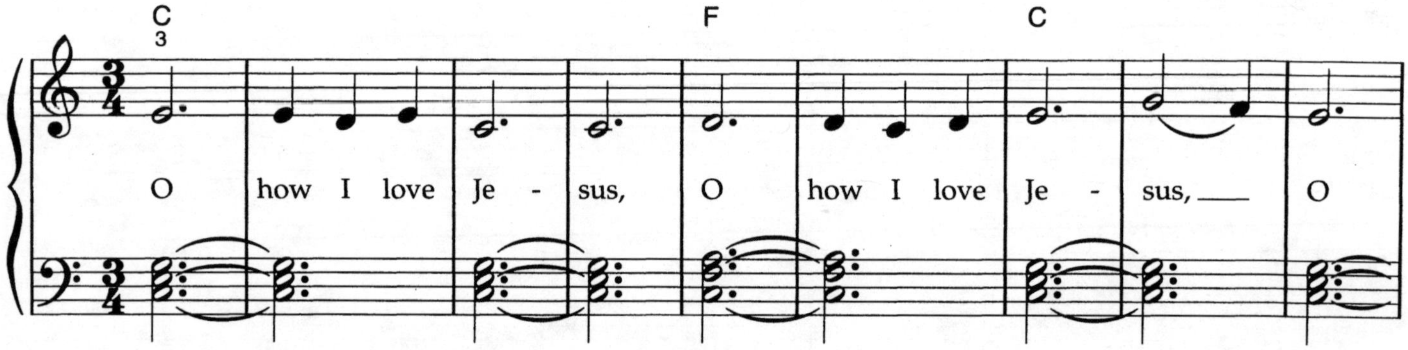
C
3
F
C
O how I love Je - sus, O how I love Je - sus, O

G7
C
how I love Je - sus, be - cause He first loved me.

ONWARD, CHRISTIAN SOLDIERS

SABINE BARING-GOULD

ARTHUR S. SULLIVAN
Arranged by CAROLE FLATAU

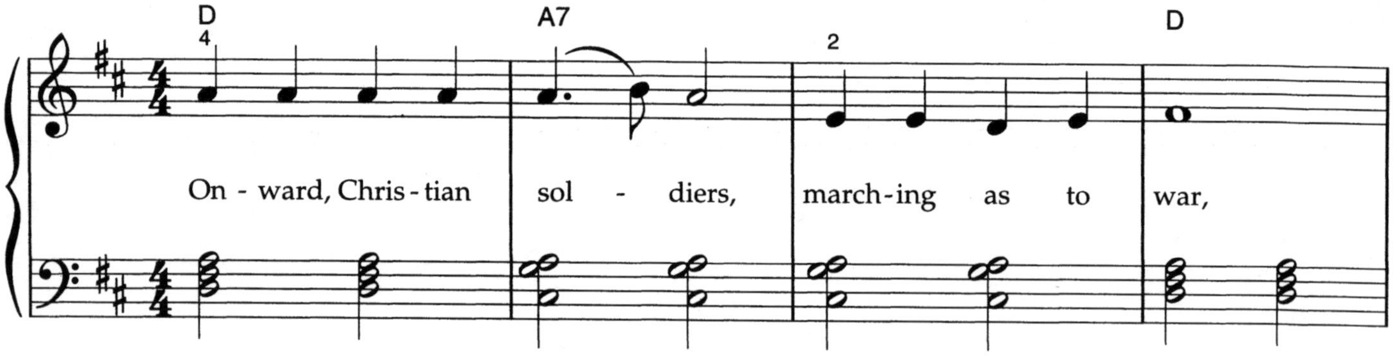
D
4
A7
2
D
On - ward, Chris - tian sol - diers, march - ing as to war,

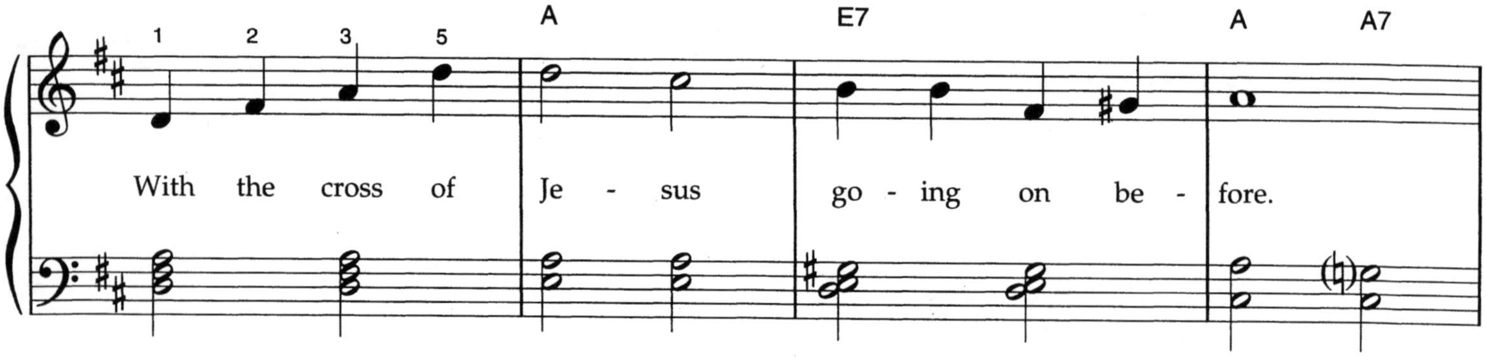
1 2 3 5
A
E7
A
A7
With the cross of Je - sus go - ing on be - fore.

D G
Christ, the roy - al Mas - ter leads a - gainst the foe;
A7
For - ward in - to bat - tle ___ see His ban - ner go.
CHORUS
D A7 D
On - ward, Chris - tian sol - diers, ___ march - ing as to ___ war,
A7 D A7 D
With the cross of Je - sus go - ing on be - fore!
8va

O WORSHIP THE KING

ROBERT GRANT

J. MICHAEL HAYDN
Arranged by CAROLE FLATAU

G C D7
O wor - ship the King, All glo - rious a - bove, O
G D7 G
grate - ful - ly sing His pow - er and His love. Our
D D7
shield and de - fend - er, The an - cient of days, Pa -
G Em D7 G
vil - ioned in splen - dor And gird - ed with praise.

STAND UP, STAND UP FOR JESUS

GEORGE DUFFIELD

GEORGE J. WEBB
Arranged by CAROLE FLATAU

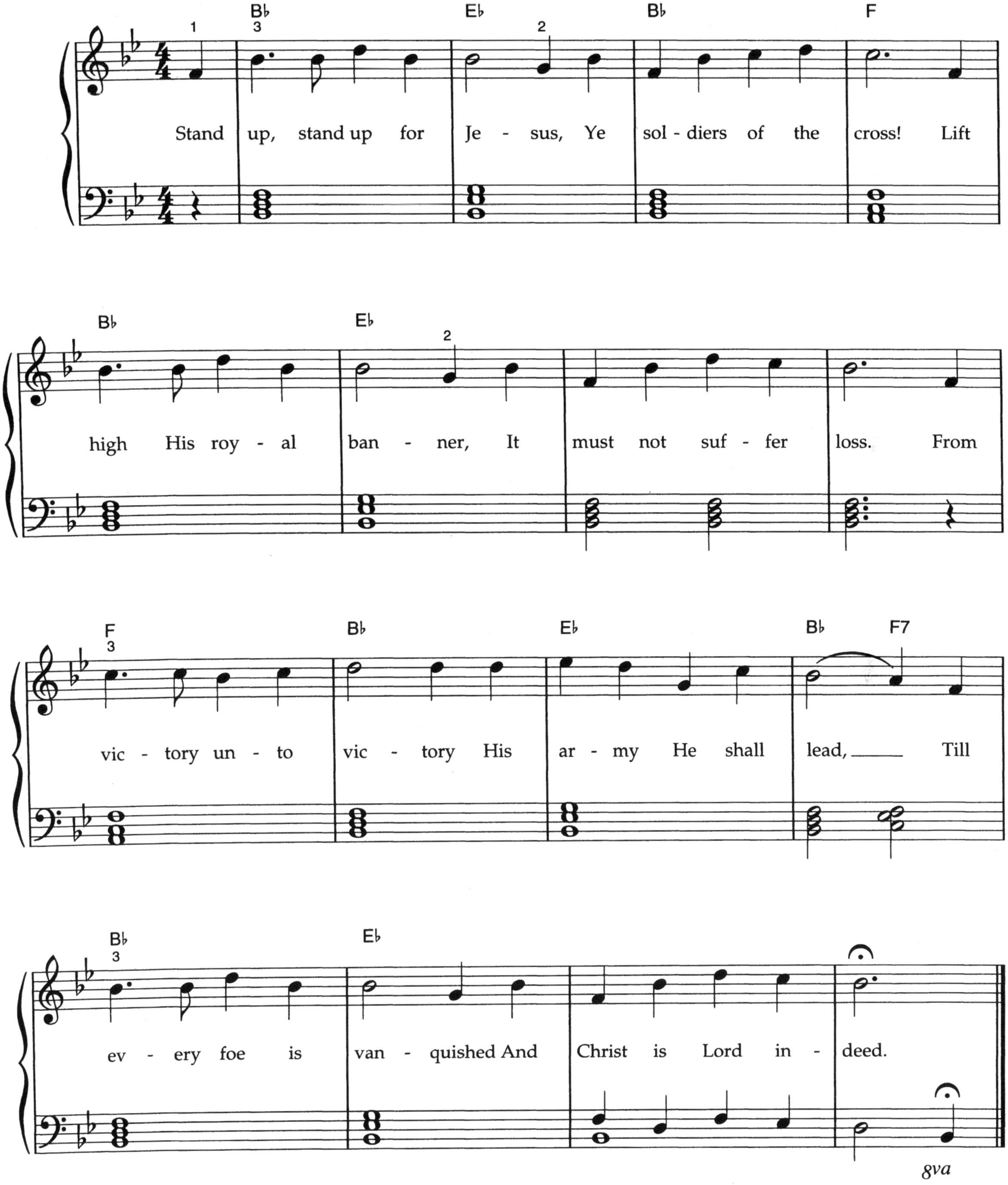
B♭ E♭ B♭ F
Stand up, stand up for Je - sus, Ye sol - diers of the cross! Lift
B♭ E♭
high His roy - al ban - ner, It must not suf - fer loss. From
F B♭ E♭ B♭ F7
vic - tory un - to vic - tory His ar - my He shall lead, Till
B♭ E♭
ev - ery foe is van - quished And Christ is Lord in - deed.
8va

SUN OF MY SOUL

KATHOLISCHES GESANGBUGH
Arranged by CAROLE FLATAU

F
2
C7
F
Sun of my soul Thou Sav - ior dear,
3
C7
It is not night if Thou be near;
F
O may no earth - born cloud a - rise
B♭
5
F
C7
1
F
2
To hide Thee from Thy serv - ant's eyes.

SWEET HOUR OF PRAYER

W.W. WALFORD

WILLIAM BRADBURY
Arranged by CAROLE FLATAU

C F C
Sweet hour of prayer, sweet hour of prayer, That calls me from _ a
G C F
world of care, And bids me at my Fa - ther's throne, Make
C G C F
all my wants _ and wish - es known. In sea - sons of dis -
C F C G7 C
tress and grief, My soul has oft - en found re - lief, And oft es -
F C G7 C
caped the temp - ter's snare By thy re - turn, _ sweet hour of prayer.

THIS IS MY FATHER'S WORLD

M.D. BABCOCK

FRANKLIN SHEPPARD
Arranged by CAROLE FLATAU

D G A7
This is my Fa - ther's world, And to my list - 'ning ears All
D A7 D
na - ture sings, and 'round me rings The mu - sic of the spheres. This
G D
is my Fa - ther's world! I rest me in the thought Of
A7 D
rocks and trees, of skies and seas, His hand the won - ders wrought.

THIS IS THE DAY

Psalm 118

TRADITIONAL
Arranged by CAROLE FLATAU

C
1
G7
This is the day, this is the day that the Lord has made, that the
1
Lord has made, I will re - joice, I will re - joice and be
C
F
4
glad in it, and be glad in it. This is the day that the
C
1 2 1
F
4
C
1 2 1
Lord has made, I will re - joice and be glad in it.
G7 C
This is the day, this is the day that the Lord has made.

WE GATHER TOGETHER

NETHERLANDS FOLK SONG
Arranged by CAROLE FLATAU

C G7 C
We gath - er to - geth - er to ask the Lord's bless - ing, He
G D7 G
chast - ens and hast - ens His will to make known. The
G7 C G7 C
wick - ed op - press - ing now cease them from dis - tress - ing; Sing
F C G7 C
prais - es to His name, He for - gets not His own.

WHAT A FRIEND WE HAVE IN JESUS

JOSEPH SCRIVEN

CHARLES CONVERSE
Arranged by CAROLE FLATAU

F Bb F C
What a Friend we have in Je - sus, All our sins and griefs to bear.
F Bb F
What a priv - i - lege to car - ry Ev - 'ry - thing to God in prayer.
C F Bb F C
Oh, what peace we oft - en for - feit, Oh, what need-less pain we bear,
F F
All be-cause we do not car - ry Ev - 'ry - thing to God in prayer.

WHEN HE COMETH

WILLIAM CUSHING

GEORGE F. ROOT
Arranged by CAROLE FLATAU

C G7
When He com - eth, when He com - eth To make up His
C G7 C
jew - els, All His jew - els, pre-cious jew - els, His loved and His own.
CHORUS
F C
Like the stars of the morn - ing, His bright crown a -
F C G7 C
dorn - ing, They shall shine in their beau - ty, bright gems for His crown.

Alfred